Heart Marketing

Engaging with your Ideal Customer

through Marketing Philosophies that Matter

Shane McLeay

#heartmarketing

DEDICATION

I really need to thank all my mentors that have shared their wisdom and invested into my life, you know who you are. Without your guidance, patience, wisdom and commitment this book would never have happened and so I say thank you.

To my amazing clients who entrust me with their incredible stories, I say to you that it has been an incredible honour and privilege.

To my beautiful girls, Ellie and Lilly, thank you for keeping me grounded and for your patience throughout this project, the next book is for you.

Lastly, I would like to dedicate this book to you the reader. May it help bring you back to that place in your business from where you can understand the heart of your customer and engage with them at that meaningful level.

With gratitude.

Shane

CONTENTS

Step 1
YOUR WHY

Start with your Why and rediscover the heart behind your passion?

Tell your story - The why behind what you do.

In the world of marketing so much emphasis is placed on data and numbers that it becomes easy to forget who we are really trying to reach.

Let's forget the numbers and data just for a while and focus on the heart of who you want to reach with the message of your why.

The reason you do what you do in your business. Let's look at how you can communicate the story of your business and the story of what it is that really matters.

One thing that is fundamental in marketing, is that the only reason you are marketing, is to reach and connect with individuals that you want as your customers or clients, a point that is often lost in the business world today.

In this world of government compliance, technology overload and distraction, it can be so easy to forget that your audience are real people who have real hopes and real dreams and that's what you need to be speaking to.

Marketing or branding strategies based on sheets of data is the cold, impersonal, outdated way, of strategising and building a marketing campaign. These old world ideas and approaches belong in the ego driven corporate boardrooms of the world, not in a business with heart and soul, that wants to make a difference.

Sure, numbers and data have their place in reporting and in preparing strategies, however if you base your entire marketing strategy around this old world mindset, you will be less effective in engaging the market, spend more on marketing and have fewer brand ambassadors working on your behalf.

If you can change your approach in your marketing and be more intentional about who you want to speak to and have clarity in the message you send to the marketplace, you will indeed change the dynamics of your business.

The great news today is that you have a powerful marketing opportunity right before you and that is your story. The things that make you who you are as a brand. The people you want to speak to through your marketing activities are people just like you and I, they have dreams, hopes, visions and a value system that will help them align with something they believe in or something they are passionate about, whether that be a brand, a cause or a feeling.

Always remember to consider the heart of your ideal customer and treat them with respect and they will respond to your message as it resonates within them.

Now is a good time to look back on what you've been doing with your marketing and focus on where you are now and where you really want to be.

Think about the future and how you can communicate your message to the marketplace and think deeply about who it is you are really trying to reach through your marketing and what it is you are wanting to say to them.

The real secret to success in marketing, in this new age, is to engage the market at the very heart.

To engage the heart of the person that you want to reach, is how you will stand apart in the new millennium.

The world has changed and so has the marketplace. When you can truly understand the heart of the individual that you want to reach and engage with, it is then that you can tell your story directly to them and engage them in the most effective way.

Knowing the heart of your ideal customer is powerful, speak to the heart and you will always make a powerful connection. Listen with your heart and you will hear what other can't.

Speaking to the heart will give you an advantage, when you know who you want to speak to, why you want to speak to them and how to share your story with them.

To engage hearts and minds through the story telling process is as old as humanity itself, many of our earliest memories are based around stories being read to us. Corporations, like Disney make enormous amounts of money every year from telling stories. Entire cultures and religions only exist today because of storytelling, myths and legends. They exist through effective story telling that captures the imagination and more importantly the heart.

You have probably heard it said that there's nothing new under the sun, it has also been said that there is nothing new in advertising and marketing either and this may well be the case for those who have never discovered their unique place in the world. There is one thing that is new and fresh in this world of recycled originality that you may have overlooked or downplayed and that is your story. It's never been told before, it's original and it's yours.

The world isn't looking for another copy of Starbucks or another Elvis Presley, be original and be you, because who you are and what you bring to this world is amazing and this world is looking for unique and amazing, it's looking for you.

In all of history, there has never been another you, so what you bring through your story and what you project through your enthusiasm and energy is unique. This from a marketing and branding perspective, is incredibly powerful so don't waste it and don't surrender it because only you can own it.

We live in an age, that is starved of unique stories and brands, individuals are longing for something or someone to connect with. Something they can identify with, something they can feel a part of and belong to. Something they can pour their hearts and souls into.

Your unique story is your greatest asset when it comes to marketing. Your story is your passport to greater things. Stand out from the crowd and create something real and fresh that will engage the people you want to connect with by telling your story.

The world will take notice of you because they are waiting for more of what's real and are ready to reject less of what's not.

In the noise and clutter of marketing messages in the world today, people are looking for things that make them feel real and human again.

Never forget, that the people you are trying to reach are just like you and me. Engage with their hopes, dreams and visions and give them a reason to align themselves with your brand.

If you can offer hope through your story and what you have overcome or achieved and innovated, you will become someone's hero. The world is short on real hero's today.

We are living in a time like never before in the history of known humanity, individuals are relentlessly bombarded with marketing messages trying to sell and convince them constantly. People are becoming increasingly overwhelmed by the noise and they just want to turn off. The passion and energy that flows from your story will cut through the shallow marketing campaigns that the big corporations deliver, giving you a real advantage.

I have learnt two foundational lessons on this journey and they are that

1. you can't fake sincerity and

2. you can't buy integrity.

Coming to the market place with these two qualities intact is extremely powerful and will provide a solid foundation for the future. Tell your story and be real because there are so many people who want what's real and their thirst is rarely quenched.

If you are taking the time to read this book, then there is a very good chance that you are passionate about what you do, you are most likely committed to self improvement, education and you believe in what it is that you are doing. You have purpose and you have a destination in mind.

If you are a person that is committed to becoming better than the person you were yesterday, then I am certain you have a story to tell.

The passion within you can be channeled and projected into telling your story. Opening doorways into the outcomes you want to see.

The passion that lies within you, is the fuel that will drive you to new heights. This passion will capture the hearts and minds of those you wish to engage with and it will speak to them when they hear your story. All you need to do is be real.

Within you, dwells greatness, and out of the greatness that you possess flows your story. Much of that greatness is found within the why. The why being the passionate reason that you do what you do on a daily basis. It is your why that will inspire and captivate those you want to reach, converting them into your customers and if you treat them well, your brand ambassadors.

Tell your story as openly and as honestly as you possibly can, speak to the heart of your ideal customer, not their head.

Speak to their dreams, their hopes and be who you truly are. Open up to the marketplace about what drives you. People see not just with their eyes, so communicate your story with them in truth.

If it's not you fronting your brand, ensure that whoever is representing your brand reflects and embraces the core values of what your brand represents and communicates those values well.

The why, as in the why you do what you do, is what you are really bringing to the marketplace. Your why is the message that every aspect of your marketing and branding should be established upon.

Once you have established the why as your solid foundation, you can begin building the remainder of your marketing and branding on this platform.

People really do care about the reasons why you do what you do, when it aligns with their core values.

If you have failed to identify and communicate the why in your business or brand you really are missing an amazing opportunity to grow your business.

Without the why you are simply a copycat version of something someone else has said or done in the past.

If you are feeling a little lost in your marketing journey stop and remember the why.

Ask yourself, why do I do what I do?

_____

_____

_____

_____

_____

_____

_____

_____

Why did you start or purchase your business or brand?

_____

_____

_____

_____

What was the deciding factor behind you embarking on your business journey?

_____

_____

_____

_____

These are important questions and they may take some time and some soul searching to answer. If you are honest with yourself, rediscovering your why can be one of the most liberating and powerful exercises you can ever undertake in the life of your business.

In the busyness of life, it can be easy to forget why you wanted to start your business journey. If you're just starting out, your passion and energy levels are most likely high, capture that energy right now and make it count.

Maybe you have been striving for so long and reached a point of exhaustion where you feel as though you are wasting your time, energy and money. Maybe you feel as though you have lost your way, maybe you are potentially giving business away to your competitors without even knowing it, simply because you have forgotten, never understood or applied the "why" to your marketing.

The good news is that all of the above are what almost every entrepreneur has experienced at some point in time and there is hope.

By taking the time to discover or rediscover the elements of your why and what makes you truly unique, will establish you as an engaging leader in your field. Passion always shines brighter than someone who is simply going through the motions. There are tens of thousands of great marketing ideas that have come and gone over the years, but there is no better strategy than discovering the philosophy behind the what, why and how of your story, start building this into an original concept for your brand and ongoing marketing.

Be courageous, be smart, be you and above all else operate in truth. Your story, your why - is your unique point of difference.

If you are communicating your why with your customer, you are going to draw the ideal customer directly to you through passion, engagement and by establishing a real heart connection.

No one can tell your story like you can. No one knows your story like you do. Tell your story to the world, tell it every day and tell it to whoever will listen but do it intelligently with a well thought out strategy, through a targeted delivery system.

To help refresh your memory reflect on the questions below:

What is the reason that makes you get up every day and do what you do?

_____

_____

_____

What are the core values around what you do, why are they important?

_____

_____

_____

_____

_____

_____

_____

What is it that you do or offer that makes a difference in the world?

_____

_____

_____

_____

Why would people care about what you do?

_____

_____

_____

_____

Through the hardest times in your business, what gave you strength and kept you going, why did you push on?

_____

_____

_____

If you could tell your ideal customer in one sentence why they should engage with you, what would that sentence say?

_____

_____

_____

_____

Your responses to the above questions will help you establish or remember why you do what you do and why you can tell your story to the waiting market.

When you have a sound understanding of the why behind what it is that you do, you will always be ready to respond to the marketplace.

In marketing, there are fundamental principles that never change, for example people generally buy from those who they know, like and trust and when they see passion and conviction in your story they will be drawn to your brand, to your product and to your message.

Tell your story with sincerity and with integrity, your potential customers and clients are tired of being over sold. Tired of being lied to and misled. People are tired of gimmicks and they are tired of being manipulated.

People will pay good money for good services and products that reflect their values and core beliefs, from brands that they know, like and trust. Through the telling of your story they will come to know you, like you and trust you.

The world is longing to connect with what's real. Consumers are having their intelligence insulted on a daily basis by over the top "clever" advertising campaigns that often fail to truly engage the marketplace. They are either offensive, irrelevant, un-engaging or simply a reactive, quick fix to address the need to have a marketing strategy in place.

These campaigns work, simply due to the enormous amount of dollars poured into them and the carpet bombing strategies that are implemented for their delivery.

These companies could save huge sums of money, if they simply stopped and listened to the market and to the one they actually want to talk to.

Social media, reality TV and talk back radio shows have all grown their audience numbers because there is an element of perceived reality attached to these offerings. This is what people want today.

Even though these programs are anything but real and are highly edited and controlled, people are so hungry for a taste of what's real. They engage with these programming formats and platforms.

Reality TV will generally be focused around the telling of someone's story. Talk back radio is generally based around an individual's story or experience and social media is people telling their stories for the world to see, sometimes too much of their story.

This "reality fix", gives people a behind the scenes look at what was once otherwise mysterious or even forbidden, lifting the veil on what was, enabling them to become part of the story.

You only have to look at the television show Goggle Box to see a good example of this. People watching people watch TV - who would of thought. To be honest, it's pretty sad that this is what our culture has become, however for the purpose of this book we are wanting to reach people where they are. Sadly - this space is where many of them can be found.

People don't always want the rehearsed and the pre-meditated. They often want the real and the spontaneous. Ultimately, they want the whole truth and nothing but the truth (until it makes them uncomfortable or challenges their world view).

Why you do what you do is your story. Your why is the reality that people are wanting to connect with. Now more than ever before, it is so easy to tell your story in so many ways and through countless delivery systems that will carry your message to your ideal customer.

The world is waiting to hear from you, they are ready to listen. The question that you need to ask yourself is this: are you ready to speak with them? Are you truly ready to engage with them and share your unique story with them?

In everything you do be original and ensure you reflect the values of your brand and your why. Everything you are projecting from product packaging, logo and brand design, wording, through to media placement and delivery, should tell of your why.

Remember, your story is unique and no one else can own your story. This is empowering because all of a sudden you are on an equal footing with the big players of the business world.

You can now sit at the same table as the "movers and shakers", when it comes to marketing your business, I can assure you, that a passionate business owner who knows and understands their why can achieve so much more cut through and engagement than someone who is simply spending shareholders' money on a polished marketing campaign or the business owner who is simply ticking boxes.

A really productive exercise is to write down on a single page, in as much detail as possible, the why behind what it is you do. You can use your answers to the questions on the previous pages to help you complete this exercise.

One of my old mentors once told me, the truth is always with you, you only ever have to prepare lies.

People want truth and transparency, don't let fear of those who might like to pull you down, deter you from this valuable exercise. Your critics and naysayers will only have power over you while ever you give it to them.

You don't need anyone else's permission to live your life and pursue your goals and dreams. You certainly don't need their approval to tell your story and be you.

You are not in business to achieve mediocracy, but to soar to levels of greatness. The level of greatness that you decide upon, not someone else's idea of what greatness is. Mediocracy doesn't really require a lot of effort. It just happens. A lot of the time, it can happen even when your sights are set on greatness.

In a world of mediocre mindsets, it is very refreshing to know that the mountain peaks are still within reach for those prepared to make the climb. Those who are prepared to do what others won't.

These mountain peaks don't always come to you, sometimes you have to go to them and you have to climb them. One step, then the next, you can do it.

It might be interesting to note here, that the only time a mountain will come to you is during an avalanche or earthquake. Don't wait for the mountain to fall on you, conquer it first.

Mediocracy will rob you of what's rightfully yours. It is dangerous, it can consume you without warning, it can impact on your marketing activities and infect the entire culture of your business. You don't want mediocracy to be your "why", you don't want any part of it in your business or indeed your life.

Sadly, for the vast majority, greatness is nothing more than a dream or a fleeting wish. Greatness means different things to different people. For those who are prepared to dig deep, and tread where others fear and do what others won't, will experience their moment of greatness.

We each walk a unique path, that said, there are universal principles that are consistent on the path to success and those that understand these principles will always have an advantage in the marketplace.

What's all this got to do with marketing and telling your story, you might ask?

Everything!

The mindset you bring to your business and the why really are the determining factors, governing how your journey will unfold. What it will look like, how it will feel and where it will end. For most entrepreneurs, your business really is an extension of you, birthed out of your vision for a better way of doing things or an experience, that is better than what the marketplace was already experiencing. For many, this is their why.

If you want to be serious about marketing and if you really want to leave behind the nothingness of mediocracy, then you need to explore the deep places that make you who you are and the philosophies behind what it is that sets you apart as a business.

Arrive at that place that enables you to have a strong sense of what it is that makes you who you are, this knowledge will see you stand out from your competitors, you need to know your why and understand your own story before anyone else will get it.

What is the greatness that lies within your brand?

This greatness is birthed in your why, the why being your mindset and the underlying philosophies that were established within your business from its inception until now.

Having a coffee shop with your only wow element being that you have air conditioning, unfortunately places you in the zone of "so what" and mediocracy in the marketplace.

Having a coffee shop with a designer coffee menu that changes every month, because that's a part of your why, is far more exciting than "come on in, we're air conditioned" or "come on in, we sell coffee". I would be more curious about a Chilli Bean Java Dream than air conditioning.

Your why element soon becomes your WOW element, when you

identify it and understand its importance in the grand scheme of things.

WOW is what engages the heart, not mediocracy.

There comes a time in every business where the opportunity to rise to greatness is closer than most can ever comprehend. I know that somewhere in your business there is a Chilli Bean Java Dream, just waiting to be discovered. The old saying "people don't buy what you do, they buy why you do it", is as true now as the day that saying was coined. Today this idea holds more relevance than ever before.

Mediocracy and greatness have one thing in common. They are both chosen by us. It's one or the other - you choose.

Take the time to understand your why. Your why is the philosophy that everything you do should be built upon.

Are these "why" philosophies established in your business and more importantly are these philosophies alive and well today in your business? Is the culture of your business reflecting the philosophy behind what you do each and every day and more importantly are you?

If I looked at your logo, your colour scheme, your website, your

TV commercial, your YouTube channel, will I see your why reflected in what you do? Will I know your story? Will you engage and capture my attention? Will it engage my heart?

You can watch, read, attend, subscribe to and devour, all the mindset and marketing content there is to devour, but if you won't change what you're doing now, nothing in your future will change.

All the knowledge, motivation and wisdom in the world will mean nothing unless you apply it and take action.

Do you want to be exactly where you are now, weeks, months or years from today?

Reconnect with the passion and philosophies that got you started. Rediscover your greatness today. Remember them every day, live your why, for this is your story of greatness, the story that the marketplace is longing to hear.

A really honest and confronting question to ask yourself is this. Do you believe in your own story enough, to take that story to the world and ask the waiting marketplace if they want to become a part of your evolving story?

People want to know what the benefit is for THEM. If they buy from you and not your competitor, you had better have a very good reason as to why, because if you can't explain to them the reason why, you can be sure that your competitors will.

It all comes back to educating your potential customers through the art of storytelling.

If you can't passionately communicate to someone why you do what you do in business and what your brand is all about, can I submit to you that you revisit the why behind what you are doing.

People will respond to the energy and emotion in your passion. I once heard emotion described as energy in motion. This emotion in your story is a critical ingredient to any captivating marketing strategy.

SHANE'S TIP

Marketing isn't about what you're selling. It's about what you're telling. Tell the right story - your story and growth will follow. If you choose to do the hard sell up front, it can easily undermine your marketing efforts. People are tired of being sold to, stop trying to sell to everyone and start talking instead, this is how you build long term relationships. Build a relationship and you will build a customer for the long term.

Step 2
YOUR BUDGET

What is your budget?

You don't have a budget, do you?

Throughout my business and marketing career I have met countless business owners who were proud of the fact that they didn't spend a cent on marketing, I have had business owners boast to me about how much money they had saved by not spending on advertising or marketing. Sadly, most of them are no longer in business today.

Marketing isn't a way of getting rid of money with no projected return. Intelligent marketing is a proven vehicle, that drives your business and increases your turnover, throughout the life of your business.

Ultimately the result of marketing should see an increase in your market share and your profit margins.

If experience has taught me one thing, it is that a negative or reckless attitude towards marketing, usually leads to one common outcome. That being, a severe and negative impact on business and longevity.

I have asked so many business owners and managers over the years, what their marketing budget has been only to receive a blank stare followed by a series of ummm's and err's. My response - "you don't have a marketing budget, do you?"

Your marketing budget matters just as much as your sales budget and every other budget in your business.

Having a marketing budget is the second step in an effective marketing strategy. Without it, you are headed for disaster.

If you don't have a marketing budget in place, you will either over or under invest in marketing and make poorer decisions.

Establishing a marketing budget isn't hard. If you don't have one, now is a really good time to establish one.

Depending on the industry you are in, it can be relatively easy to set a marketing budget based on historical or projected turnover. Look at the benchmarks within your industry and then decide if your budget should be more or less. Only you will know what is sustainable and realistic.

Many suppliers you deal with also have cooperative marketing funds available to support their proactive dealers or partners. All you need to do is submit a marketing plan with real costings and projections and you will be surprised at what you can achieve. The old saying "if you don't ask you don't get" is alive and well. So invest focused thought and energy into how you can create a proposal for your suppliers to secure some marketing funding.

One problem that exists today in the business world, is that the marketing dollar is often treated with very little respect from business owners or managers.

Your marketing dollars are an investment in your business and in your brand. Ultimately in your long term future.

A big mistake people make is that they give marketing budgets no real attention and wonder why their marketing activities fail.

Understanding that your marketing dollars are an investment in your business and indeed your future will enable you to shift the view you have around your marketing.

A marketing budget will disappear very quickly if it isn't subject to a well thought out marketing strategy. Knowing what you have to invest and where it will be invested, well in advance, will result in a much greater outcome for you. In other words, have a plan not just a budget.

Whenever you are considering your marketing budget you have to be fully aware of the outcomes you are wanting to achieve.

Are you simply in a branding phase in your business where you just want to get your story out to the marketplace or are you looking for call to action campaigns?

These questions are very relevant and impact on establishing your marketing budget. Different activities require different budgets. Consider having a branding budget and a call to action/sale budget to boost sales and enquiries in quieter times.

Another benefit of having a definitive marketing budget, coupled with a minimum twelve month marketing strategy is that media executives will treat you with much more respect. They will be increasingly mindful in what they present to you and assume that you are more savvy. In turn they will be more focused on what advice and pricing they are offering you.

In a world where trillions of dollars are often carelessly spent on advertising and marketing every year, you need to ensure that the budget you have allocated to your marketing has a clearly defined purpose with a projected outcome. This is one of the greatest pieces of marketing wisdom I can communicate to you. Your attitude toward your marketing budget will ultimately determine the success of your marketing activities.

Be very clear in your mind about why your marketing budget is there and what it needs to achieve. Always refer back to your marketing strategy and your marketing budget on a regular basis and be accountable.

Remember, don't be afraid of your marketing budget - be responsible for it and it will reward you.

SHANE'S TIP

Be intentional about your marketing budget and understand the investment required and the time it will take to see results. Be proactive not reactive and if you need help then ask for it from a credible, independent source and remember to stay within your budget.

Step 3
YOUR CUSTOMER

Who do you want as your customer?

How is your one dimensional view of your customer working for you?

For the last 30 - 40 years' media companies have been educating you about demographics and data. Instead of teaching you that the key to real marketing is getting to know the heart of your customer.

Get to know your customer by name and understand what makes them tick.

Get to know your ideal customer as an individual, this is the smart way to market and by far, the most cost effective strategy.

Have you ever wanted to sack half of your customers and get better ones?

I think I might know the answer to that question. So why not do it?

So many companies and brands have been marketing so broadly that they have managed to end up with so many unwanted and difficult customers that its detrimental to their business.

Not every customer is beneficial to your big picture. Some customers cost you money and time creating a negative impact on your brand.

The sad but liberating truth here is that some customers aren't worth having. The trouble is that more often than not, we get what we ask for. So often we aren't being specific in what we are asking for, ending up with a customer base we never really wanted.

Another way to think about this, is who do you want to spend your time with?

Who do you really want to focus on as a customer? Who are the types of people you like spending time with?

Imagine a customer base that you actually like, so many business people I speak to, constantly complain about whinging and difficult customers, yet they invest their marketing resources in attracting them.

Decide on who your ideal customer is and market towards them. Speak to them, engage with them at a heart level and you will build quality relationships with them for the long term.

How much money are you wasting by marketing to the wrong people?

One of the biggest mistakes made in the business world today is the enormous amount of money that is unnecessarily wasted because business (both small and large) don't really know who their ideal customer is. They believe that every customer is a good customer.

There has never been a better time to market your message to the individual you want to reach, than now. With the customer profiling tools available, the vast social media platforms, mass media marketing options and direct marketing options, all you really need to do is know your customer. I'm talking about the individual you really want to have as your customer.

A trap so many business people fall into, is the idea that that they need to reach and speak to the entire marketplace to be successful. Nothing could be further from the truth for most businesses.

I'm pretty sure, that a life insurance company would not want to be speaking to an individual who is on life support, or someone in their seventies. No more than a weight loss company would want to be speaking to fit and healthy people.

The time, energy and resources you will invest in identifying your ideal customer, will reap immeasurable dividends over a very long period of time. So knowing your customer and building a strong, long term relationship with them should be one of your highest priorities.

Who is your customer?

_____
_____
_____
_____
_____
_____
_____

What makes them tick?

_____
_____
_____
_____

Remember that people aren't just numbers on some marketing data spread sheet. People are individuals with real needs, real dreams, real goals and real wants and you need to engage them at a heart level.

Where does your customer "hang out"?

_____
_____
_____
_____

What do they do to relax?

_____

_____

_____

_____

Would finance options appeal to them and enable them to purchase your products and services?

What is the one emotive message that you can deliver to your potential customer that will cause them to connect with your brand or product?

What do you need to do to keep them connected at the heart level?

If you are spending all your marketing budget on trying to talk to the people who will only buy from you when you are on sale then you are going to find it difficult to ever reach your potential in business.

How much of your budget is talking to the internet buyer who would rather save $10 online? Are they the customer you really want?

In a world that is often about greed and selfishness you can still build strong and enduring relationships in business that will stand the test of time and technology. It's about marrying your unique story with your budget, your ideal customer and then your delivery strategy.

Whenever you are marketing, whatever you are marketing and whoever you are marketing to, you need to be fully aware that every time you are targeting an individual, you are really targeting two people. The person that they are and the person they really want to be. Know who they are in their heart of hearts.

Without the human trait of always wanting more many industries would fade away. One thing that has driven consumerism and marketing is the understanding that people want to be somebody else. They want to feel different and they will do whatever they can to achieve this outcome.

That said, knowing the heart of the real person you need to target is key to a successful outcome, once you reach the real person you can hone in on who they want to be and how they want to feel.

Retail chain Victoria's Secret has an intimate, in-depth understanding of who their perfect customer is. To reach this understanding they created a profile that was approximately 40 pages thick outlining who that perfect customer is. In this profile, they know how much she earns, what her buying patterns are, what sort of vehicle she drives, her favourite TV programs, what she cooks for dinner, her favourite music and so on.

This report was based around a fictional character who is given the name Victoria and the marketing people at Victoria's Secret marketed directly to this fictional character because she represented their perfect customer. She was the target individual that they wanted to market to. What an intelligent and cost effective strategy!

By creating this profile Victoria's Secret understood what made Victoria unique; they knew her priorities, her political persuasions, her fundamental beliefs and they understood what Victoria wanted and needed as a consumer. All of their marketing strategies and efforts were focused on her wants and needs.

Successful companies like Victoria's Secret know that the better you can understand your customer, the more effective they will be at reaching them and engaging them with their message.

In a nutshell, they took the time to understand the desires of Victoria's heart and then market directly to them.

Knowing your customer is absolutely key to any business that wants to grow.

What is the demographic of your customer?

_____

_____

_____

_____

What is their age, their income, where do they live?

_____

_____

_____

_____

What is the psychological makeup of your customer?

_____

_____

_____

_____

What are their values?

_____

_____

_____

_____

Are they motivated by environmental issues?

_____

_____

What are the behavioural habits of your customer?

_____

_____

_____

_____

_____

_____

What is their product usage?

_____

_____

_____

_____

What do they buy from you?

_____

_____

_____

_____

How often do they buy from you?

_____

_____

_____

_____

Do they price shop you?

_____

_____

_____

_____

_____

Do they only buy from you when you are on sale?

_____

_____

_____

Do they refer you to their friends and family and if so how?

_____

_____

_____

_____

Do they watch television?

_____
_____
_____
_____

Do they read magazines?

_____
_____

Are they addicted to social media platforms?

_____
_____
_____
_____

Where are you going to find them?

_____
_____
_____
_____

If you want to make the effort to know who your customer really is, then you will reap the rewards of that effort.

Before you market to your customer knowing what his or her

needs and wants are, will increase your marketing effectiveness. When you know what he or she wants you to know what to offer them and how to communicate and engage with them at a heart level.

When you know who your customer is, everything from packaging through to colour schemes and advertising strategies are all geared to that person, rather than trying to speak to a broad sector.

It costs a lot of money to speak to the masses but it costs very little to speak to an individual - food for thought.

Some of the most successful businesses in their respective categories have focused on creating relationships with their potential and existing customers by placing an emphasis on building an emotional connection with them because they know it works.

You can start to engage your target market today by discovering what makes them tick and market towards that motivating impulse.

Know the desire, understand the heart and engage the customer.

Get personal with your customer, know them, speak directly to them when you are marketing and treat them with respect, sure – joke with them but always treat them with respect.

You will never build a successful brand if you fail to focus on the customer, because no matter how good your logo is, how user friendly your website is or how big your marketing budget might be, without your customer, you have nothing, so it's a good idea to get it right. Find out who they are and treat them with respect.

If you are marketing to everyone, then you really are marketing to no one. You need to focus in on your desired customer and know exactly who they are as an individual and know how to reach them.

Let's take a look at why a potential customer might choose to do business or make a purchase from you?

Is it because your product represents greater value or superior quality?

Is it because you have worked hard to find designer products?

Is it because you service the brands you sell, giving your potential customers piece of mind?

If you know the reasons why, you will know how to speak even more directly to your customer. Knowledge really is power in marketing and power in marketing is the lifeblood of success.

If out of all your existing customers, you can hone in on those you would like more of and ask them why they choose your product or brand, they will be able to provide valuable insight into their "why". Understanding why your customer makes certain decisions is just as important as understanding how you can provide them with the solutions they want and need.

Finding the answers to the above questions, will give you enormous leverage when it comes to engaging with the marketplace. The real benefit here is that when you know who it is you are really trying to reach; your marketing dollar becomes so much more effective.

Marketing today requires a greater personal approach and a unique message tailored towards the specific person or the niche you want to reach.

Understanding this principle will enhance your position in the marketplace. Having the ability to speak directly to your customer is true engagement. While ever you have direct engagement with an individual, do you think that your competitors have a chance of muscling in? Not likely.

In marketing folk lore there is a story about a business owner who was asked about his marketing effectiveness. He is asked which part of his marketing works best and the business owner responds by saying that only half works but he doesn't know which half.

Imagine if you took the time and effort to refine your message and target in on who you really want your customer to be. It would be a lot easier to know where your wasted marketing dollars were going and how to bring change to the outcome.

Do you really know why your existing customers are buying from you?

Do you know why those that aren't your customers don't buy from you?

Take the time to find out the answers to these questions and watch your sales increase when you actively address these issues.

Are you brave enough to survey your customers and ask them for their honest feedback? If you are, the information they provide could transform your business.

Knowing exactly who you are trying to reach is a huge advantage. When zeroing in on these people you should be reminding them about the real points of difference that you offer the market. Tell them over and over the unique points that make you who you are.

McDonalds and Hungry Jacks sell exactly the same products but they attract different customers, why is that?

Don't get me wrong here, I know that we all need a flow of customers and I don't negate that. However a question I really see as valid, is how much time and money do you waste, trying to get the wrong customer into your business?

Why compromise your long term vision, just to make a sale?

Real estate is a great example. One thing is for sure in real estate, you can never have too much market share. This is a classic example of an industry that really needs to be in touch with its big picture strategy and the heart of the customer.

One on one engagement with the marketplace is a key element to the existence of a real estate agent. Ultimately, it's all about building and maintaining a relationship with tomorrows buyer long before they know that they will need a real estate agent.

A property is a property and if selling properties is what you do, you need to be very clear about your point of difference as an agent. All real estate agents list and sell properties.

Focus on the big picture strategies and make sure you are marketing to the heart of your ideal customer because you really need to be engaging them.

Your strategy is the vehicle that will drive you way beyond your competitors and knowing your big picture strategy will keep you on track in a world filled with competitors who have no targeted heart engaging strategies.

In real estate, knowing the heart of your customer is absolutely powerful. The beautiful thing about this scenario is that etched deep in the heart of hearts of humanity, everyone wants to feel like they are home. That they are safe and provide a warm, loving environment for their family. Market to the heart of your ideal customer.

If you are a real estate agent then it is you and your team and how you market your properties and business that is your real point of difference. You are unique, so market those unique elements in an engaging way. Speak to the heart of your ideal customer. No other estate agent in town has your individual team members, your experience, your rental list, your local knowledge, your networks, relationships, your vibe and so on. Market the unique elements of your agency and be passionate about it, but above all else always remember the heart of your customer.

These same ideas can translate to industries like law and accounting, all accountants crunch numbers… all lawyers litigate.

Who do you want as your client?

Are only 7 percent of your clients your ideal client and if so why?

What message did you deliver to the marketplace that attracted the other ninety three percent?

Food for thought and a strong reminder that everything you do in marketing, is building your client base, so what are you really building?

An intelligent approach really is needed when it comes to identifying your ideal customer. A heart approach. Once this is done you can then build a solid long term relationship with your customer.

It's always a lot easier to communicate with someone that you have a relationship with, so build relationships.

Take the time to know your clients at a heart level and have a clear understanding of who it really is that you want as a client. Know them by heart.

What motivates them, what are they passionate about. What moves them to tears? Your perfect customers are waiting for you to speak to them.

SHANE'S TIP

Get to know your customers at a heart level! Get personal with them, understand them, be sincere and show them how much they mean to your business. Do what it takes to focus in on who you want to be dealing with as your perfect customer and be intentional.

Step 4
YOUR EXPECTATIONS

Most people have unrealistic expectations in Marketing.

Who wants to double their growth over the next 3 years?

To deliver a poor message or to use an insufficient marketing budget and expect great results is extremely unrealistic.

You will only ever get out of your marketing activities what you actually put in. As it is with everything else in life, your level of investment will influence your outcome. It's not just money, it's the time you invest and other resources as well.

This is why you need to have a long term plan whenever you are thinking about your marketing strategy. Remember that long term marketing strategies produce long term results, good and bad.

The marketing activity you do today, will have an impact on your business five, ten or even thirty years into the future. So ensure that the impact is positive.

Your marketing strategies need to be in total harmony with your business values, goals and the underlying philosophy behind what you do. Ultimately your marketing strategy is what steers the direction of your business and creates how people feel about your brand in the marketplace.

Your marketing strategy needs to clearly identify what makes you different or unique from your competitors. This is what is known in marketing as a differentiation strategy.

You really need to understand how you are going to communicate your point of difference to your target market and create your unique position. Take a minute to answer this question; what can I do to really engage with my ideal customer? It doesn't have to be complex, it's just got to be real and your marketing strategy needs to be in total alignment with your core values as a brand. Yes, I said it again and for a good reason.

Potential consumers want to know what makes you different from everyone else.

"Me too" marketing is a waste of time and money. In other word, telling the market place the same things your competitors are telling them with no point of difference is copycat, "me too" marketing, that no one cares about. It certainly falls short of engaging the heart.

When it comes to communicating your story and what your brand truly represents - get it right and do it well. Engage with a Marketing Consultant and dig deep into the why behind what you do.

If you don't know your own brands position in the market and its unique point of difference, how do you expect your potential customers to know?

A real estate brand's greatest potential, rests in its ability to capture the hearts and minds of those yet to sell their properties or those who are future purchasers.

The smart real estate brands, market towards these people through emotive and engaging strategies, a long time before these people have even considered listing or purchasing a property.

The real estate agent who is engaging with and connecting to the heart of their potential customers in the market do this because they know that being front and centre of the potential customer's mind gives them an incredible advantage over their competitors who don't occupy that headspace in the waiting market.

If a real estate agent ran a marketing campaign today with the expectation of creating high levels of enquiry, it would be a big ask. Especially if they had neglected marketing to future purchasers.

To expect results from the market without ever building a relationship with the people in the market is positioning your brand for failure.

Industries like real estate, law and end of life businesses, need to be engaging with the market, long before the marketplace ever requires their services.

People will turn to these services in a time of need and they will be influenced by what their understanding of a particular brand is and how it sits within their perception of the marketplace.

Smith, Baker, Slack and Associates Law Firm who never market themselves will be hard pressed to have any influence within the marketplace and can really only rely on their circle of influence for limited market penetration.

I have said it before and I will say it again, if you want the market to take you seriously, then take your position in the marketplace seriously.

Build your brand and influence the market, speak to the heart of the market and be intentional about what you offer and the outcomes you can provide.

Every tall building is built by digging deep first, lots of earth needs to be removed, before a foundation can be laid. Building a successful marketing strategy is no different, get your foundation right before you start building.

Marketing can be a black hole that you just keep pouring money into, if you don't know what you are doing. So you need to know the outcomes you want and need to see before you do anything else.

Every marketing campaign, regardless of the industry you are in, should be built on a desired outcome and vision for the future of your brand.

Like any voyage, knowing how you are going to get to the destination is the key to a successful journey. When it comes to marketing you often need to make some strong and courageous decisions. It will be these decisions that determine your future and lead you to your final destination as a brand.

It's so important to have a real plan and a sound understanding of how you are going to get to the destination. It's important to remember, the reason most businesses fail is because they don't have a comprehensive plan in place and no road map.

All the excitement and belief in an idea won't pay the bills. There is more to creating a successful business than a concept, you need substance and to have substance you need to be intentional and above all else teachable and committed to the outcome you want to see.

Let's say that you sell coffee – so what! So does McDonalds, Hungry Jacks, KFC, Starbucks, and every service station and café you drive past.

The idea of opening a business is one thing, building the emotive bridge that connects you to the marketplace is something else.

Why should I or anyone else buy coffee from you?

_____

_____

_____

_____

What will my experience be?

_____

_____

_____

_____

Do you have the unrealistic expectation that just because you sell coffee I'm going to buy it?

If you want the marketplace to take your business or brand seriously, then you really need to consider how you view the marketplace and your position in it.

The idea of selling coffee is not enough, coffee will only ever be a part of the experience.

What is the emotive reason, the wow factor that will make me buy your coffee and keep me coming back over and over again?

The answer to this question will decide the success or failure of your business.

Are the outcomes you are expecting to see, truly reflective of the investment you have made in time, resources, energy and money? Or are your expectations unrealistic based more on wishful thinking, than real effort?

Creativity and new ideas are great however they are never, ever enough.

Make your business an experience, tell your story and involve your customer in that story.

Give them something tangible, give them the experience that they will want to come back for. It doesn't need to be over the top, it simply needs to be real and it needs to engage them at a heart level.

By knowing your customer as an individual, you have the very real opportunity to increase not only your business turnover but your profitability. As well, simply because you no longer need to market to the masses, knowing your customer before you commence your marketing campaign, will contribute to a much higher success rate.

If a business has grown or even just survived by simply ticking boxes and advertising, imagine the benefits and increase that will come from an intentional marketing strategy.

By focusing in on your business and having a big picture view of where you want to be, by integrating your vision with your marketing strategy, you could potentially double your turnover within the next three years. What would that mean to you as an individual?

How much closer to where you long to be, would a result like that place you on your journey?

Very few people are here to work or to just build a business. For most people their business is the vehicle that will enable them to reach a higher place.

Most of us have dreams that are really important to us. Dreams that we want to see become realities. So what we do today, really does matter and what we do today does have a massive impact on where we arrive tomorrow.

It's for this reason we really need to be focused and intentional, on our marketing. Our marketing is the road map for where we will arrive whether intentionally or unintentionally.

There is a principle that I have come to live by and it makes a lot of sense and it is this. The place where you decide to focus your intention is important, it is from this place that your outcomes will flow. It is from this flow that your dreams become reality.

In other words, where you focus your intention, attention and energy combined, at this point all things begin to unfold and manifest. Be very deliberate and clear when it comes to your intentions and know the consequences and understand the potential outcomes.

This is not only true for marketing and business but life in general, many of the lessons in business and marketing have their origins founded deeply in the spiritual principles of life.

To connect with the heart of an individual means we are also connecting with the real them… the spirit and essence of who they are.

When it comes to successful marketing, understand that the TV, radio or social media campaigns really are the final stages. What is going to ensure success for you is what happens within your business and your marketing long before your campaigns are launched.

We know that all television, radio, magazine, social media and all other delivery systems work, so if you commence a campaign that doesn't work, it wasn't the delivery system, it was the strategy or the content that failed.

In my experience the main reasons marketing campaigns fail are:

No strategic planning: don't do anything unless you have a plan. The plan needs to have a starting point, a budget, it needs to cover who you want to reach and it needs to have an end date and a projected realistic outcome.

Poor content: your content which really is your story, needs to be delivered clearly and to a high standard. The best graphic design or production crew on the planet will mean nothing, if your message is vague, soft or confusing, so spend the time to get it right.

Unclear message: again, be really clear about your message. It needs to come from your story. Let people know the outcomes of what you do and how it will resonate with them. Let them see how your offering will help them achieve their hopes and dreams.

Insufficient budget to carry out the strategy: Don't make the mistake of trying to cover too many platforms with a small budget. Do one thing and do it well. Build your audience through one medium at a time and when you have consistency and engagement in one, you can expand your budget and your delivery strategy.

Poor timing: Make sure your timing is right and doesn't conflict with something that could take away from your campaign. Be sensitive to what's going on in the news. An honest mistake or poor timing can do a lot of damage to your brand.

Lack of preparation: Coming up with your ad copy or production brief three days before the launch date of your campaign isn't the best of strategies. The truth is, you are better off postponing your campaign and getting it right, than going to the market with a substandard message.

Poor targeting: Know who you want to speak to and design your entire campaign to that individual, remember Victoria Secret's profile on Vicki? Be very intentional about where your placement and energies are focused.

We all make mistakes, we all fail and we will all continue to do so. It's called being human. To suggest that you're never going to make a mistake again in your marketing, is a tad unrealistic and a little bit arrogant. To understand that it's ok to make a mistake is actually very liberating and it's how we learn. The important thing is that we do actually learn from our mistakes. Learning from our mistakes makes us better at our craft.

The biggest mistake you can make in your marketing is to have unrealistic expectations about your outcomes. Be real and understand, what it is that you can actually achieve with the resources you have.

SHANE'S TIP

Your marketing plan is as equally important as your financial plan. They should sit side by side and work hand in hand. If you don't have a marketing plan, you really need to create one. Your total business plan is the roadmap to your businesses future and ultimately its success. Without these fundamental plans in place, failure will often be the final outcome.

Step 5
YOUR STORY

Turning your Story into an engaging message that will cut through and reach your ideal customer.

If you're not front and mind of your potential customers thought process you have already failed.

Gaining the attention of the marketplace isn't easy. So be authentic in communicating your story to the marketplace in a way that captures their attention.

Create engagement and earn the respect of those you are wanting to connect with. This is the path to a successful outcome.

We have been told by the sales gurus of the twentieth century to "sell the sizzle, not the sausage". It goes a lot further than just selling the sizzle in the twenty first century.

The sizzle is the idea around how they will feel if they buy your product, the sausage are the tangible benefits and outcomes that come as a result of buying your product.

What we as marketers need to remember is that the market is over being sold empty sizzles… they want the sausage. Sure, sell the sizzle, but make sure you remember to sell the sausage as well. Your customer will do enough sizzling for you in the marketplace, as a result of being treated with respect and integrity and arriving at the outcome they wanted or needed.

Meet or exceed a customer's expectations and you will create loyalty in your brand or message. Once a customer knows and trusts you as a brand they will be more receptive to your messages in future and they will respond quicker. This is why marketing should be a constant exercise.

The truth is that you can't fake sincerity. You can't buy integrity. So never compromise these two things in your business at any level. Especially in your marketing.

Building your marketing message on a foundation of truth and integrity is smart and it pays off.

You never want to create a negative stigma around your business that is based in lies, mistruths or empty promises - leave those mistakes to your competitors.

Let's look at coffee again and the idea around selling coffee and how simply offering coffee is not enough.

Coffee will only ever be a part of the overall experience. Sure your coffee might taste good but why in an abundance of coffee outlets am I going to come to you for your coffee?

What is the emotive reason that will make me buy your coffee and keep me coming back?

Whether its coffee or fashion, you have to know the answer to this question. The answer lies in engaging me at a heart level.

If I love your coffee why would I go anywhere else?

If I love the way I'm greeted in your coffee shop and the atmosphere and experience you offer, why would I go anywhere else?

Make me fall in love with what you do and I will keep coming back, it's really that simple.

I use coffee as an example for the simple reason that it perfectly demonstrates how something so readily available in the market place can be delivered in so many different ways and on so many different levels.

Think about your favourite coffee shop or restaurant. What is it that makes you want to go back there?

What are the things you love about it?

What are the things that make you feel comfortable, happy and welcomed?

How have they captured your heart?

The answer can be found in the little things and in the big things. It's all about the overall experience.

My fourteen-year-old daughter Ellie, is living proof that a brand, when marketed effectively and targeted to the ideal customer can influence even those who have never experienced, touched, tasted or tried the product.

Given Ellie's age she obviously isn't a seasoned coffee drinker nor has she ever been in a Starbucks outlet. The nearest Starbucks is approximately 370 kilometres away from our home.

All that said, Ellie is a real ambassador for Starbucks, she has been planning a family weekend away, all of which revolves around a visit to Starbucks. She can even tell me what their logo means and where it came from. What's on their menu and how they write your name on a coffee cup and call your name out when your order is ready.

That my friends, is the power of incredible story telling in marketing and that is how you build a brand.

How did she become so obsessed with the Starbuck's brand you might ask? A YouTuber she watches is also obsessed with the

Starbuck's brand and so brand evangelism is working very well for Starbucks via social media.

Social media platforms are extremely powerful, if used correctly and should never be underestimated. If you are looking to engage with the marketplace and aren't on social media today you really aren't anywhere.

Starbucks are the largest coffee retailers on the planet and have succeeded in reaching into the hearts and minds of their target market. People who buy from Starbuck's know that they aren't just a food or coffee outlet. They have positioned themselves to be a feel good destination and they have all the boxes ticked when it comes to creating a brand that really has become a stand-alone culture, in a world of countless competitors all vying for market share in the coffee industry.

Starbucks are certainly more than a coffee shop that sells muffins and wraps. They have created a strong brand that is more about being a culture than a food chain. They have learned how to engage the hearts and minds of their customers giving them an experience – not just a coffee.

Starbucks have mastered the ability to engage in an ongoing conversation with their customer. Giving them the ability through a loyal relationship to constantly communicate whatever it is they want to communicate to their waiting and trusting audience.

From a marketing and branding point of view it doesn't get much better than the Starbucks story.

I can almost hear you saying "Hey, I can't do that! I'm not Starbucks!", I'm here to assure you, that yes you can.

Any brand can break down barriers, cross cultural boundaries and influence all ages, when a successful and achievable marketing strategy has been executed. Execution of the strategy should be followed by consistency and frequency. Remember, even Starbucks had to start somewhere and you do to.

None of what we are talking about here is out of reach for you and your business. Start at the beginning with what you have and build from that place.

Grain by grain a loaf, brick by brick a castle. Build from one marketing success to the next and to the next, this is how businesses grow and this is how success is nurtured and sustained.

Sadly, there are no guarantees when it comes to marketing and countless ideas have failed, due to poor planning and a lack of commitment on the part of those who were responsible for the outcomes. Even the best marketers in the world today can fall short. It's about being consistent and always being there in the hearts and minds of the market.

If your brand is going to exist ten years from now and be thriving, you need to see today where you want your brand to be in a decade's time. Not only do you need to see it but you need to relentlessly market towards the outcome you desire.

It is possible to bring an unknown brand into the marketplace today and grow its market share very quickly. You just need to know your plan and strategy.

The only way your brand will succeed in today's competitive world and reach its true potential, is to be committed to its success with determination and passion.

You have to remain committed to the realistic outcome that is your hearts vision. Taking a measured risk for a measured gain. The vision that was established in your heart must be protected and nurtured. This is how you build success.

The world is full of businesses and marketing strategies that have failed because they were prematurely abandoned. To see success in a marketing strategy means you have to see it through to completion.

A marketing strategy that hasn't been given the opportunity to run its course will rarely deliver the results you desire. Be committed to the outcome and your heart's vision and you will truly thrive.

You need to be innovative with your marketing. If you can't be innovative to the level that is required, then go find someone who can be.

Engage with someone who has credibility, a proven track record and understands your brand. Someone who understands where you want to be.

Marketing your brand and your offering is one of the most fundamental aspects of your business strategy and it should always be treated with the respect it deserves and needs. Please take your marketing seriously, it matters.

Imagine if McDonalds or Jeep took their focus off their marketing strategies. It wouldn't take long for their competitors to move in for the kill and show no mercy in the process.

I have seen firsthand, what happens when a company makes a marketing blunder. Their competitors will miraculously find the marketing dollars needed to gain the advantage from their error. Unfortunately, it can be very nasty out there.

You have to know your plan, you need to be familiar with every detail of your strategy and most importantly follow it through to completion.

If you are serious about what it is you want to achieve and have a solid, intelligent plan, you will remain committed and faithful to the outcome − no matter what the cost.

None of this is complicated, turning your story into an engaging message is as easy as communicating what it is that you do, why you are doing it, and focusing in on the passion you have. Then the real secret is to effectively communicate those elements to the heart of your potential customer.

If you are a photographer and the biggest kick you get is from a family capturing beautiful memories from a moment in time, then tell that story.

Explain that what you do isn't about taking photos, you are capturing treasured memories that will last a lifetime. No one in consumer land cares about your technique or the type of camera you use. They want to know that their treasured memories are safe in your hands.

If you are a funeral home most people won't care that you are family owned. So what! If that's your pitch, it's all about you and not the families.

How are you going to help me say good bye to my loved one?

How are you going to get me through the most difficult time I might ever face?

Why should I turn to you?

What qualifies you to take care of my loved one?

There is a beautiful saying I once heard and it goes like this. "People don't care how much you know until they know how much you care".

These are important elements to consider in your marketing, especially if you are dealing in sensitive industries like end of life or the legal and financial sectors.

It doesn't matter how sensitive the industry is that you are in you still need to reach the heart of the customer.

If you're selling doors it's still about the heart of the person you are trying to reach. You aren't selling a door, you are providing safety and security to someone's house and you are helping them make their house a home. This is the key to successful marketing. You are helping them fulfil their dream, it's never just a door.

Your story is forever unfolding. It isn't set in stone and for those that understand this, you will have a real advantage in the marketplace because you know that there is always something new and fresh to be talking about. All of which is focused on your story and based in the passion for what it is that you do.

If your marketing strategy is built on the story of you then your marketing is a living thing - how exciting.

Tell your story based around outcomes. The outcomes that your potential clients want to see and experience. Let's look at a couple of ideas below:

Dentists don't sell drilling or fillings - they offer pain relief and beautiful smiles.

Airlines don't sell rides on planes - they offer beautiful destinations or reunions with loved ones around the world.

Pet Shops don't sell pets - they offer loving companions.

Computer retailers don't sell tech gear - they provide you with the tools and technology you need to achieve your dreams.

Nurseries don't sell plants - they help you create a paradise in your own back yard.

Pest Controllers don't spray poison around your house to kill harmful pests - they offer peace of mind for your family and property, providing protection for the most important things in your life.

Apply this idea to your marketing and you will soar.

SHANE'S TIP

Tell your story the way that feels the most natural for you. Be creative, be courageous but above all else be real, be sincere and remember to speak to the heart of your potential customer.

Step 6

YOUR DELIVERY SYSTEM

If you know who your customer is, you will know where they hang out and how to reach them.

Becoming intimate with your customers.

Buying ads on the radio, commercials on TV, ads on social media, the internet or the newspaper is not marketing. These are all simply delivery systems for a message. It is heartbreaking to see businesses, both small and large waste large sums of money on ineffective advertising campaigns that have nothing to do with communicating their story to their customer. Resulting in underperforming campaigns and unrealistic expectations.

Your brand is an asset and every time you market your brand the end result should be that you are building and adding value to your asset.

Creating an effective marketing message and then delivering that message to your target audience is critical to the survival and longevity of your brand.

Your marketing is the line you draw in the sand that defines your position in the marketplace. It builds defence against your competitors and delivered effectively, it will transform people into your fans and brand ambassadors.

Ask yourself this question, how many customers do you lose to competitors simply because they don't know what it is you really offer or deliver?

So many marketing messages today are nothing more than an idea someone thought was "clever" in a corporate boardroom and these messages say very little and waste thousands of dollars.

In marketing we know that people buy from brands that they know like and trust, does the market know, like and trust you?

In a crowded marketplace, it's almost impossible to make enough noise to be heard above the anthems of clever jingles, fancy websites, clever logo's and the absolute bombardment of the airwaves, press and internet, that is really nothing more than marketing clutter.

The important question to ask here is this. When you do make a noise, what are you saying and who are you saying it to?

How do you get amongst the noise and more importantly be heard? The first thing to do as I mentioned previously, is to live and breathe your marketing strategy and completely understand it. There is no other way. I will keep repeating the message, that if you don't know who you are, where you sit in the marketplace, who your customer is and what makes you unique then how will your potential customer ever know?

Keeping your message simple is the key to gaining your potential customers attention, there is no point in explaining the scientific formula behind your product and marketing that message, if you can't engage with and grab the attention of your target customer in the first place.

For the most part a consumer with dry and flaky skin really doesn't care about the scientific formula behind a product, they just want their dry and flaky skin to go away, it's about the outcome. They want to hear about the solution, then and only then, if they are interested they might look into the formula.

Every business is unique and has a story to tell, so when you are developing your marketing messages be mindful not to inundate your potential customers by trying to cram your entire story into one message.

One message at a time, will reap you results. Again, keep it simple, keep it focused and make it frequent.

Above all, keep it aligned with your big picture marketing strategy and your values.

Don't over complicate your message with boring facts that are a back story to the overall purpose of your marketing campaign. The quickest way to sabotage a marketing strategy is to bore the marketplace with things you think are important that really aren't.

I see a large number of campaigns waste enormous amounts of money because the advertiser gets all caught up in the technical nothingness of their product. Ending up with a blah blah blah message that very few people will want to listen to.

People are for the most part like goldfish, they have short attention spans and we know that in the world today you have less than five seconds before a potential customer tunes out of your advertising message.

As a matter of interest this timeframe is about the same for people landing on a website. If they aren't engaged or comfortable with your site or message within approximately five seconds you have lost them. They leave and look elsewhere, so you really need to focus on being real and relevant and engaging them as soon as possible.

Another classic way to waste your marketing budget is to tell everyone how good your service is. That my friend, is only your opinion and when attempting to connect to people who don't know your product or brand you can have all the service in the world, but if they don't understand what you do you have gone into blah blah blah mode. Let's face it, who is going to say that their service is bad?

Want to know something else?

Your service is supposed to be excellent. That is a minimum expectation from anyone who is contemplating doing business with you. If good or excellent service is your only story you are in serious trouble.

If you believe that your service is amazing and superior to your competitors don't build your marketing campaign around that idea. Most people won't believe you anyway.

I laugh when my eleven-year-old daughter Lilly is watching TV or listening to the radio and a substandard commercial comes on. She will mock the ad, as if to make the statement "do you really expect me to believe that?".

I smile and remind her that she is a very smart girl and that if she can differentiate a good marketing message from a bad one at her age then she has a great career waiting for her in the marketing world of the future.

I mention Lilly for a reason, if you can't fool Lilly as an eleven year old, how will you convince a more mature audience, that are your potential customer?

The standout point here is to be mindful of the message that you are delivering to the market and how you are delivering it.

A great way to talk about your product or services, is to use quality testimonial ads. Use real customers talking about real experiences based upon their real history and relationship with your brand. This is a great way to communicate an important part of what your story truly is.

A testimonial is often more believable and can be more engaging than a cookie cutter ad produced with a voice over artist. Please do it right and use the right people. You don't want to be a security company using the biggest ex-con in town endorsing your brand or a healthy café using unhealthy, overweight people as brand ambassadors.

In marketing, you really need to think before you act and then when you think you've got it, think again. Getting your story right and delivering it to the heart of your target audience is what really matters.

Everything you do impacts on your brand and everything that impacts on your brand impacts on your future. It's important to understand what you are doing, the why behind it and above all else be real in all that you do.

Put thought into how the marketplace will respond to what you are putting out there. Remember – it should be simple, easy to understand and above all, it should be real and it most certainly should be the truth.

Imagine a high profile business owner who has a fleet of vehicles explaining why his fleet is serviced by a specific mechanical repair business. His endorsement is pure gold to the mechanical shop and his network of friends and business associates will be influenced by his endorsement.

Testimonials really work when they are approached with integrity and sincerity, in other words, when they are real.

One success story is a campaign I developed with Peter Bolte, a successful electrical appliance retailer. We really drilled down to build a campaign that would speak directly to the individual, Peter wanted to reach and because of his personality and integrity, I insisted we do a series of television commercials where he fronted the camera, explaining his offering and experience. These were used alongside customer testimonials and the category we targeted saw record sales and a real and measurable return on his marketing investment.

All that said, the strategy we used with Peter Bolte won't work in every situation and like everything it can be overdone.

If in doubt about a specific strategy always go back to your big picture marketing plan and if your idea doesn't fit with the big picture plan, then there is a good chance that it's not the right direction for you to take.

Marketing for the sake of marketing is pointless, don't do it! If your target customer reads your brochure, sees your ad or looks at your logo and thinks "so what" then you have failed.

You don't want to be a "so what" brand! You need to be as good at marketing as you possibly can be and better at it than your competitors. You need to align yourself with smart marketers who get it and preferably those with proven experience and an unbiased view of the delivery options available to you.

I know from experience that in the grand scheme of things it takes very little effort to lift the performance of an average business and see real results in a relatively short period of time. However I do know that it does take a commitment of time, energy and resources.

It's frustrating to see how many business owners neglect marketing and freely hand over tens of thousands of dollars if not millions to their competitors without giving it a thought. Simply by settling for substandard marketing practices.

Even though for a lot of his business life, Colonel Sanders of the Kentucky Fried Chicken fame, may not have been a raging success, his later years yielded some real genius. Instead of rolling out blah blah blah marketing messages, he publicly marketed the fact that his recipe for fried chicken was a secret and he wasn't going to tell you.

This was clever, while everyone else was making noise, Colonel Sanders' noise was very different and it worked. His message was essentially "you can buy my chicken, but I'm not telling you what's in it", he created intrigue.

Some industries are harder to market than others. Let's look at the funeral industry as an example. The funeral industry can appear difficult to market on the surface because no one wants to talk about death and dying.

For the most part we live in a culture that is in total denial, when it comes to death and many will avoid the subject at all costs.

Remember this, for most people, death is scary and it is feared. People don't want to talk about it and in turn they often don't know what to do when that time comes.

This is the mindset of the person, a funeral home is really marketing to.

No matter what business you are in you, must know who it is you are actually marketing to. How they are thinking and where their heart is.

Being a great funeral director does not make you a great marketer. A lot of marketing people are often out of touch with what the funeral industry is really all about. So if you are outsourcing your marketing, make sure the person you are outsourcing to has a sound understanding of your industry and the sensitivity surrounding what it is that you do.

I recently heard a funeral radio ad making light of the subject of death and dying. Someone, somewhere, probably thought it would get a laugh. Humour is great, we all need to laugh, but not at the expense of alienating a large number of your audience.

Treat your customers with respect, be the solution to their fears, problems and concerns.

When you provide a service or product that really doesn't have a tangible aspect to it, you have a challenge ahead and you need to work hard to engage with your market and create desire.

People don't talk much about funerals in general but if a funeral home delivers a bad funeral or if the florist delivers the wrong coloured flowers, they will never hear the end of it from their customer.

There may not be a desire for a funeral in the consumers mind today, however there will always be a need and an expectation for a high standard from a funeral provider. Defining what a successful funeral is, will vary depending on who you are talking to.

It's a tough gig but one thing is for sure - we are all going to be the customer of a funeral home one day.

The question to ask now is what are the influencing factors that will determine which funeral home gets your funeral?

Write those responses down and then apply those things to your business and how your customers might feel about what you have to offer.

I can assure you that in the funeral industry the majority of families that a funeral home engages with, wants to be treated with dignity, respect, empathy and compassion. So in the marketing strategy, these elements must be recognised and addressed.

They want to know that the funeral directors are professionals who operate with sensitivity, not standing around outside the chapel telling jokes, laughing or texting on their phones.

Remember, everything you do is creating a perception in the marketplace and in the digital age you really are under the microscope.

Successful marketing results come when you know exactly who you are speaking to. So it is important in industries like the funeral industry, to know who it is they should be speaking to.

Is it the fifty year old who has great health or is it the eighty year old who has great health?

The eighty year old may or may not have made arrangements with a funeral home, so enter the next of kin, fifty year old who will have influence in which funeral home will get the business, if no prior arrangements have been made.

Decide who you want to be speaking to in this scenario and market to that individual. speak to the fifty old influencer if that is who you want as your ideal customer or speak to the older parent, it's your choice but please speak to someone and engage with them at the heart level.

Knowing how to speak to your customer is a lot easier when you know who your customer is. When you know who your customer is, you know what it is you need to communicate to them?

What do they need to hear from you and how do they want to feel after hearing from you?

These are all important questions that need to be answered by you before you begin to market.

Build your story to engage with the heart of your customer and deliver your message in a way that will give you the attention you deserve.

An effective approach for an industry like the funeral industry would be a sincere, emotional voice coming over the airwaves saying; "Jan had been sick for quite a while and when she passed away I didn't really know what to do or where to turn. I had never had to organise a funeral before but John from Smithers Family funerals helped me get through it, I really don't know what I would have done without them".

A real person with a real experience and if produced and delivered properly, it would be a cut through message engaging the listener and communicating a powerful message about trust, compassion empathy and everything we hope a funeral home would deliver in our time of need.

The sincerity of somebody's, husband, father, or grandfather... all of a sudden, it's real and its personal. All of a sudden, the listener relates and you have engaged them. You have engaged the heart of it all.

Now it's not some paid voice over artist trying to sound sincere. It's real and it hits home. It speaks to the heart.

People like real and they like sincerity and if you can get your message above the ordinary "so what" level, then you are a mile in front of your competitors.

In life, I have learned at least two very valuable lessons. The first being that you can't fake sincerity and the second being that you can't buy integrity.

Integrity and sincerity should be foundational in life and equally, so in marketing. It doesn't matter what you are selling or promoting or what position you take in presenting your message, if it isn't grounded in sincerity and integrity then you are kidding yourself and the people you are trying to reach. They will see straight through your insincerity and your lack of integrity, costing you and your brand greatly.

If you think I'm being conservative or overly cautious, you may have missed the point, the most aggressive and successful skate and surf brands in the world today have built their brands on trust, integrity and sincerity along with a hell of a lot of attitude.

These companies know that their customers will walk away from their brands if they compromise on quality or betray the cultures that the brands are supposed to represent.

In the consumers mind, it's all about what a brand stands for and how it makes them feel when they are associated with that brand, it's about values. Substandard "so what", "blah blah" marketing is a danger to the brand image and all that it stands for.

When someone wants to look, and feel a certain way by wearing a particular skate or surf brand on their t-shirt, the integrity of that brand is everything. If that integrity is compromised in any way, the brand loyalist will most likely drop their support when their values become unaligned or threatened.

Remember, image to many people is one thing they won't compromise and being aligned with a brand, that all of a sudden strays from its core values, can result in a parting of ways.

In the surf and skate industry, it's all about the image and belonging. It's a tribal thing. It's all about the feel and it's all driven by powerful yet very subtle values centred marketing that speaks with and engages the heart.

You don't rise to the top of your industry with neglectful half baked "so what" marketing strategies that don't reflect your values. You get to the top by having strong values and by being committed and intentional. This applies to every business everywhere and in every category imaginable.

In positioning and strategising your brand you must have a clear and defined understanding of what your values are and if you haven't done this then now is the time to do it.

In the space provided, write down your values as a brand:

What does your brand stand for?

_____

_____

_____

_____

What is the heart and soul of your brand?

_____

_____

_____

_____

How do you add value to the world?

_____

_____

_____

_____

What are the most important things to your brand? Are they your team? Your customers? Suppliers?

_____

_____

_____

_____

In what areas are you working hard to bring about positive and meaningful change?

_____

_____

Who is your tribe? Who are the people you believe it is most important to connect with?

_____

_____

_____

What is the one thing you would risk it all for?

_____

_____

_____

_____

What is the dream that drives you?

_____

_____

_____

Take the information you completed above and create your brands values, reflect on these daily and make sure everyone and anyone who is associated with your brand knows them - especially your team and your customers.

If you want to see a classic example of a "so what" marketing message, keep a look out for political messages, next time there is an election in the wind.

The marketing campaigns generally initiated by politicians and their parties are often fear based propaganda giving us "so what" marketing at its best. The masses tune out and who can blame them.

If only these politicians and their "marketers" truly understood marketing and what it is that people truly value. Their campaigns would be very, very different and so would the outcomes.

Knowing your customer and what they think and feel is the key to success and what's equally important is them knowing and understanding your values. If you don't like a "so what" attitude, it's a safe bet your customers won't either.

I'm sure you will agree after the 2016 US election, politicians around the world will be reassessing how they deliver their marketing messages and how they engage with their potential voters.

In his exclusive interview with 60 Minutes, Donald Trump sung the praises of social media and proclaimed how it helped him win the election. Watch this space, because it's going to be an interesting future.

A "good idea" isn't a marketing strategy. It's a good idea and many good ideas unfortunately are nothing more than opportunities to waste large sums of money.

Establish your marketing budget and take your good idea, flesh it out, and turn it into a long term marketing strategy that is based on where you want to be in the short, medium and long term. Your future really does depend upon it.

My advice to anyone who is considering commencing a marketing campaign is that before they do anything they need to look at the big picture. It's not about the postage stamp, it's about where you really want to be.

Get serious about your business and where you want to be and consider the best way to construct your marketing strategy and know how you will fund it.

Know who you want to speak to and understand how best to reach them.

Always remember that your marketing plan should be viewed as a living entity, always evolving, always growing and changing when required and ultimately – always evolving into the big picture.

Having a sound understanding of whether you should be branding or operating a call to action strategy is key to successful marketing.

If you are going to commence a branding campaign then understand it in detail before you commence it and likewise for call to action.

Now what's all this got to do with delivering your message?

Only everything!

Having your message right, is the first part of a two part process. The second step is knowing how and where to deliver your message.

Once you have profiled your ideal customer you will know how to reach them.

If your ideal customer wakes up at 6am and reaches for their phone so they can view Facebook or YouTube, you know where to reach them.

If they then turn on the radio or TV while they eat breakfast and get ready for work, you know where to reach them.

You get the idea and it goes on from there.

If you sell fishing tackle, you know already who your ideal customer is and where to reach them. A great idea would be to develop a TV campaign based around fishing programs or a weekend fishing program sponsorship on the radio.

The more you know and understand who your ideal customer is, the more effective you are at reaching them and engaging with them at a heart level.

Choose your delivery methods wisely and take your own feelings and emotions out of it.

If your ego is running the strategy, you are in trouble. Don't book ads in a TV program, just because you like the show. Base your strategy on what your ideal customer loves to watch.

Understand your customer, become intimate with them. Work on your relationship with them.

Nurture them, value them and know them - intimately.

In much of the world's marketing today. we are seeing companies literally yelling into the faces of their potential customers, trying to grab their attention. It will work as a quick fix, but it won't build longevity or intimacy.

Being present in the heart of your customer is powerful. This presence will leave those who are competing against you with outdated marketing concepts a long way behind you.

If you can understand and embrace the power of the heart, you will arrive in the place where you long to be.

There are many buzz words and trendy themes in marketing today and one of them is the idea of disruptive marketing. I'm not sure about you, but I would listen openly and with curiosity to the one who captures my attention through engaging with me at a heart level. If you disrupt me, I won't be very receptive. Disruption is invasive and shows little respect. Pursue these strategies if you must, but think of the consequences and think of the type of customer you are going to attract with such aggressive strategies.

Deliver your message to the heart and be effective in the use of your marketing budget. Whether it be television, radio, social media or any of the other options, know who you are talking to and speak to their heart.

Understand your market and understand where they spend their time and what's important to them and strategise from there.

SHANE'S TIP

Know your brand values and if something is in conflict with those values, then ask yourself, if it is the right thing to be doing? Maintaining your brand's integrity/values, is critical to the longevity of your brand.

Step 7

YOUR CLIENT

How to turn your customer into a client

On the surface the average person wouldn't really know why they shop where they shop. Most are creatures of habit. However, if you take the time to ask someone why they buy their wine at The Jolly Pirate, it will become clear that there is a strong underlying reason.

That reason could be convenience, price, range, atmosphere, environment, location, specialist in a certain spirit or it could be that they saw the ad on TV or heard it on the radio. One thing I can guarantee, is that there will be an obvious reason, no matter how subtle.

According to recent studies, it takes a minimum of twenty one days to form a new habit and if this is the case for the person who shops at The Jolly Pirate you only need to get them into your liquor store once a week for three weeks for them to consider your liquor store as a valid alternative.

Getting them into your store in the first place can often be expensive, but it's just the beginning. Now you have to convert them from a customer into a client and once you have them as a client, there is a sense of loyalty to your brand, all you need to do is keep rewarding them and exceeding their expectations.

There is a world of difference between a customer and a client and in my business, I only have clients. What's my interpretation of a customer versus a client?

The Customer

Not really loyal, wishy washy attitude when it comes to your product or offering, uses your competitors, price driven, settles for mediocre outcomes, takes short cuts, reactive in their thinking, impulsive, generally misinformed, lazy, looking for a quick fix. Just to mention some traits, ultimately no heart connection and as a result - no loyalty.

The Client

Loyalty matters. A client believes in what you do, values your relationship and experience. Price isn't an issue, as the client has a long standing relationship with you and there is trust and accountability involved on both sides. The client is committed to pre determined outcomes, purchases are considered - not impulsive, has a sound understanding of what it is you do/provide, is proactive and driven and refers friends, family and their clients to you. The client has a heart connection with you.

Who would you prefer to do business with?

The customer who is only a customer while ever they are doing business with you? They aren't really a customer again, until they choose to engage with you, if at all.

Or the client that you have an ongoing relationship with? Clients work with you for great outcomes and have a heart connection.

There is an old belief in the marketing world and that is that, it cost far less to keep an existing customer, than it does to acquire a new customer. This is so true.

Take a moment to think of your best customer and favourite people to deal with. What do they mean to your business from a monetary perspective over a twelve month period?

Write down their revenue value to your business below, then your average and worse monetary customers.

Best customer (client) value over a twelve month period:

$_____

Average customer value over a twelve month period:

$_____

Worse customer over a twelve month period:

$_____

Who do you want as your customer?

If you could nurture your average customers into clients, would you?

Ask yourself this, if you could grow an average customer into a client what impact would that have on your business over the next three years?

There are so many ways that you can create loyalty into your customer base. If you focus your energies on retaining and rewarding your clients (favourite customers) and by keeping them in the client category you will have a very healthy business.

Your secondary strategy should then be to nurture your average customers and turn them into clients as well.

Your clients will ultimately represent the stability in your business. If you manage them well, sending a client a small gift in the mail or when they come into your store or office, can mean the difference between having a happy client or a client who is a brand ambassador/evangelist.

If you sell natural skin care products, what would it cost you to send your client a lip balm and a branded T-shirt, for no reason whatsoever, other than the fact that you value them as a client.

Maximum leverage guaranteed and a stronger heart connection along with a brand ambassador who is going to tell all their friends.

If you sell coffee, ditch those tacky reward cards and take it up a notch. All of your competitors have those cards, that everyone loses or forgets so don't play follow the leader with your marketing. Create a tribe... Join The Java Tribe where you will win in a share of prizes every week, I know what I would prefer.

Creating a client out of a customer isn't hard. However, it does require focus and intention and it means speaking to the heart.

It's about creating that emotive connection, establishing the heart connection and treating your client with the respect and appreciation they deserve.

The universal principles that exist throughout the cycle of life once understood and applied to marketing are extremely powerful.

I belong to an international business network called BNI and one of the reasons I do is because of their core philosophy - that being givers gain. This philosophy and value resonates with my core values and is important to me, so they have engaged me at a heart level.

If you are working in a trade industry, like building supplies, it's amazing how much loyalty a shirt with your logo can create. Who wouldn't want their logo and brand on building sites, if you are supplying to the builders' market. These stealth strategies, are far more powerful than a TV campaign costing thousands of dollars, if your target market is a builder.

What about a dentist? What is repeat business worth to a dentist from a loyal client base of patients, who come back for regular checkups time and time again.

There is value in creating the heart connection with your customer and turning them into loyal clients.

As I always say, in business, everything you do is marketing. The way you answer the phone, how you or your staff greet a customer when they walk into your store, the music that's playing in the background, how you send out an order. It all matters and it all works together to tell the story of your brand, it's all marketing.

How will an individual feel after an interaction with your brand?

This is one of the most powerful questions you can ask yourself in relation to your where you sit in the mind of a customer.

Do you provide an underwhelming experience, is it mediocre or do you exceed your clients' expectations?

The answers to these questions all serve to show you why some people who choose to do business with you are customers and others are clients.

In the most discreet way, take one of your most average customers and make them your personal project. The project being, to turn them into one of your best clients.

Not only will this activity give you valuable insight into the amazing process of building strong relationships with a customer/client, but the experience will serve to nurture you in the revelation of what really matters in life. What really matters is the relationships that exist between you and those you value. Be they personal or professional relationships, they all require an investment of time, understanding, care and attention and that's just the beginning.

Getting to the heart of what really matters, in the customer relationship, is one of the real keys to successful and effective marketing engagement. Knowing the heart of your customer and showing them that you know this, will transform and elevate your customer into a client.

There is an old saying that goes like this, "no one cares how much you know until they know how much you care". This is absolute truth and this knowledge will give you a great deal of insight into the intricate psyche of the human condition. If you are wondering what any of this has to do with marketing, the answer is, absolutely everything.

No one cares that you sell coffee, they want the experience that you offer. Understanding that it's always about the experience, is the understanding of what it takes to turn your customers into clients.

No one cares that you sell shoes, what they care about is how they feel during the process of buying shoes from you. They want to know that if there is a problem, you will do everything in your power to remedy the situation. They want to feel confident in dealing with you, it's not about black leather and ankle straps, it is all about feeling validated during the experience of purchasing the shoes.

For many the process of buying shoes can be more about the retail therapy or the experience of feeling indulgent, than the idea of actually purchasing shoes. So if you're not creating a unique experience and tapping into the heart of your customer, you may as well send all your customers to your nearest department store or the internet.

A family who is meeting with a funeral director, generally doesn't care about the funeral directors' life experiences or what they "feel", how long they've been in business or whether or not the business is family owned. In the majority of cases, the family needs a listening ear, gentle guidance, empathy and compassion.

To focus on the heart of the customers' needs, will set you apart. Knowing why your customers have come to you and understanding the outcomes they want or need to see, is what really matters.

Your ability to understand what it is your customers really want and to deliver that expectation with intelligence and sensitivity when required, is what will set you apart. It will make you appear great in the eyes of your clients and it will save you enormous amounts of marketing dollars.

Listen to the conversations of friends and family who have just been to a new restaurant or café. Often, without even being invited, they will enthusiastically voice their opinions - good and bad.

Understanding how to tap into this human trait will provide many free marketing opportunities for your brand. All you have to do is, exceed your customers' expectations at first contact and they will be back, keep meeting and exceeding their expectations and they will no longer be customers, they will become loyal clients.

If you can win your customers heart, you will see them transform into a client. Win the heart, enjoy the outcome.

Step 8
YOUR PRICE

Price doesn't matter.

How to make price a non-issue.

Positioning yourself through Pricing

You're not in business to be a charity!

If part of your reason for being in business, is that you do want to help people from the abundance of your business, then I salute you and you have my respect. However, if you have little you can only give a little. If you have an abundance, you can give abundantly.

If you want abundance, you have to embrace an abundant mindset. You also have to value what you do and what you offer. If you value your place in the market, the marketplace will too.

We live in a very competitive world and at the very centre of this competitive culture is the idea that price is the number one influencer.

If pricing is your only offering to the marketplace, there is a serious need for you to rediscover why you are doing what you do.

Nobody wins a price war. The manufacturers and retailers don't win, because their market becomes flooded. The retailer doesn't win, because ultimately, they are sacrificing their margins, which impacts directly on their profitability and their resources.

Other than the environment, the biggest loser, is the consumer because they become partakers in a cycle that can't afford to offer them support, service, quality or satisfaction.

Yes, I understand the marketing strategy based around the idea of promoting lost leaders to increase sales and to create perception and in many cases this can be effective but it shouldn't become your standard practice.

If everything was all about price, the most popular brands on the planet today wouldn't exist.

Think about that for a second.

I use Apple products exclusively. I know I can buy cheaper devices that can do similar things. There is no way, I am going to risk, what I know works, exactly the way I want it to, for price.

Apple is rarely, if ever, on sale and that hasn't impacted on their position in the market place.

Selling two litres of milk for $2 in a supermarket, is destroying an industry and makes no sense. $2 milk is the residue of ridiculous price positioning. It's reckless. No one wins.

The individual who came up with the idea of selling $2 milk as a lost leader has now created standard pricing around milk and now nobody wins.

Real estate agents are selling unique products and to different clientele each and every day. So how do you market your brand in an often crowded space when your products and customers change so frequently?

The answer is simple, know your customer and be at the forefront of their thought process at all times. When they think property, they need to think you!

It's no different to a baker. When someone thinks bread or pastries they need to think about you and the experience you offer them, the smell of your bread when they walk near your shop, the display counter and its presentation, the free cupcake you offer them every once in a while.

If your profile and reputation are rock solid as a real estate agent the competitor who is "cheap" will never compete with you in the same arena.

Reducing your fees as an agent or working for nothing and promoting no advertising or marketing charges as a real estate agent, isn't always a positive message to send to the marketplace.

If you have instilled confidence and trust in the marketplace and proven your ability to deliver, you don't need to play the cheap game. Any smart property owner knows the maximum exposure through real estate marketing means maximum pricing and that's the outcome people want.

I wouldn't choose an agent who didn't believe in marketing my property to achieve the best possible outcome.

If you place no value on your vision, or for the sacrifices you have made in business or for your brand then position your marketing around price. You will have some success, but you won't achieve your highest potential.

If you want to be in business long after the market has forgotten about who was the cheapest then position your marketing around the story of your brand, your unique offering, your ability to deliver, your benefits, your reason why.

What is it about your brand or business that will engage the hearts of your potential customers?

What is your area of expertise or superiority?

What is the one thing that gives you an edge?

What is it that makes you different?

What is the one thing that sets you apart?

Once you have identified and communicated your one thing, you will stand out from the crowd. The crowd will listen to your message, they will want to hear and learn more about you and what makes you different.

How do you define and communicate what this one thing is?

Especially when your category is a sector like real estate?

What is the identifier that makes you stand out?

Real estate is real estate, why would a property owner choose one estate agent over another when it comes to listing a property?

Generally, its reputation, trust, perception in the marketplace, status, and the personal reputation or connection to the agent or the brand itself.

It all comes back to the heart. The trust and relationship elements that are so important to individuals, are what will give you real impact and engagement in your marketing.

The slickest marketing campaigns from the tallest glass towers in the biggest cities in the world are no match for the one who can know and understand the heart of the customer. Nothing comes close.

To really understand the irrelevance of price positioning we need to revisit the question; Who is it that you really want as your customer?

Are you really only after customers who purchase from you based on your lowest price position or are you wanting to work with quality clients who value your products and services for the long term?

Asking for $2 milk type customers is fine, if that's the type of customer you want to build your business on.

If you want longevity as a brand you won't want to be pitching to the bottom end of the market.

We all know that discounting in a one off sales event can create spikes in sales, but these are generally short lived.

The quality of customer you will attract into your business by constant discounting, will most likely end up costing you, on so many levels and for long periods of time.

Customers who don't want to pay a fair price for a product or service will usually never want to pay for things like maintenance, upgrades, accessories, time or anything else for that matter and what's worse all of the traits of a low price based customer will usually result in difficulty. The cost to you from dealing with these people, in most cases, isn't worth the aggravation.

If we look at companies like Apple, Nike or Gucci, we know that these brands didn't make it to the top of their categories by discounting their way there.

These brands listened to their customers, marketed to the heart and soul of their customers and transformed them into clients and then brand ambassadors.

All that the supermarkets (that sell milk for $2) have managed to do, is create price wars, destroy the dairy industry along with the livelihoods of those on the land and create the unrealistic expectation that two litres of milk is only worth $2.

This damaging, money grabbing strategy has leeched into other supermarket categories with the same damaging effects. Now the supermarkets are watching category profit margins erode because when one chain decides to crucify the price on a product, all their competitors follow and no one makes money.

Consumers can buy $2 milk everywhere, because the average price has been set. Irresponsible and damaging marketing that continues to achieve nothing.

If supermarkets really understood what their customers wanted they would provide an engaging experience that would reach deep into the heart of the customer and create loyalty.

There are only very few examples in the marketplace, that even come close to being an example of price integrity and customer loyalty when it comes to supermarkets.

Let's assume your product is a natural clothing range. People who want natural fibres and natural dyes, know that they are generally going to have to pay more for an environmentally sustainable product and are happy to do so. I know I will only buy bamboo, hemp or cotton clothing and this is a part of my value system. The company that provides these options and captures my attention will have a good chance of turning me into a client.

The more your product aligns with the values and the heart of your customer, the more they will support your product and maintain loyalty towards your brand.

Another great example, how you can reach the heart of your customer can be found in the bottled water industry.

Think about all the supermarket brands that discount water to the point that its almost free - another lost leader. The market is flooded (no pun intended) with water suppliers yet premium water bottlers still stand strong with branding and sound price integrity.

Voss sell water at a premium, in glass bottles and people pay for it. I know I do because I don't want the contaminants from plastic, being absorbed into my body. I will pay more for Voss because I see the value in my health and wellbeing along with the environmental benefits.

Another example of a bottled water brand is Evian. Certainly not the cheapest option available when it comes to water products yet it still performs well in the marketplace at a higher price.

Price positioning goes a long way to creating price perception. If it's $2 what's wrong with it? If it's $5 it's possibly ok and if it's $7 it has to be good! This doesn't always translate to the real world, however there is truth in the idea that pricing contributes to how a product is perceived in the market place.

Let's take a moment, right now and remember that water falls from the sky for free.

Never let yourself be convinced that people won't pay for quality products or services that resonate with their core values.

Any fuel retailer will happily sell you a coffee for a dollar when you fill up your vehicle, but a real coffee drinker will reject the one dollar option and seek out a quality coffee for up to four times the price. The answer to the question, why? Is because it's rarely about price.

So often we entertain the idea, that what we are offering isn't worthy of a certain price point because of the limitations we place on ourselves.

A realistic price that is fair and reasonable will always be welcomed in the marketplace by those who value what you are offering and why you are offering it.

It is your responsibility to educate and inform the marketplace, as to why your product should be purchased in the first place and secondly why price is irrelevant.

If you have told your story correctly you will be well on your way to positioning your product and services for a fair and reasonable price.

Let's drill down into why your product or service is valuable by answering the following questions.

1. What was the reason you first developed your product or service and why did you release it to the market, in other words - what lit the fire within you?

_____

_____

_____

_____

_____

2. What is the major benefit your product or service offers your customer?

_____

_____

_____

_____

3. How does your product or service make a difference in the world?

_____

_____

_____

4. If you had to sell your product or service to the marketplace in one sentence what would that sentence say?

_____

_____

_____

5. List the environmental benefits of your product or service below:

_____
_____
_____

6. What are the ongoing economic benefits to the end user of choosing your product or service?

_____
_____
_____
_____

7. What is the most powerful testimony you have received about your product or service and how can you extract the heart of that testimony and tell it to the world?

_____
_____
_____
_____

8. Why should I buy your product?

_____
_____
_____
_____
_____
_____

9. What is the one thing about your product that is going to reach into the heart and soul of your target customer?

_____

_____

_____

10. What is the one thing you offer that is exclusive to you?

_____

_____

_____

_____

11. How accessible is your product, where can I get it, can you deliver it directly to my door?

_____

_____

_____

_____

In the above questions, you may have had to dig a little to find the right answers. If you did, that's great.

What you now have, are all the reasons why your brand deserves premium price positioning.

If you are doubtful about your brands ability to compete in the marketplace and hold a strong pricing point then perhaps it's time to go back to the foundational reasons as to why you developed your brand, product or service and rethink. Possibly reinvent your offering until you can be confident.

You really need to believe in what you are offering the world, you have to know and understand the value of what you do beyond all reasonable doubt.

If your brand is grounded in mediocracy, then you need to rethink the mindset behind what has brought you this far.

If you don't believe that your offering has value, then go ahead and price yourself accordingly. If you see the value and benefit in what you do then believe in what you do and back yourself in every area - including price.

Two things drive human behaviour, manipulation and inspiration. Focus on inspiring your customers with inspiration and the values associated with your brand and price will soon be a much smaller issue.

Back yourself, back your brand and be intelligently patient and stay the course you have decided upon in your marketing strategy.

SHANE'S TIP

If you haven't got anything of value to say to the marketplace then don't say anything. It's better to remain silent than to deliver a "so what" message to a marketplace that expects and demands so much more than mediocracy. Remember, you will be judged by every word you deliver to the marketplace and you will be judged by the way you position your pricing to the marketplace, perception is everything.

Step 9

YOUR PAST

Learning from the Past

What worked, what didn't?

The good, the bad and the really ugly.

If what you have learnt on the journey has brought you this far, what's going to take you further?

What are you doing to get to the next level of your journey? Are you reflecting on the lessons of the past and applying those lessons to your planning and strategising?

One of the beautiful things about being human, is that we make mistakes. Mistakes are how we learn (you were wondering where the beautiful was in a mistake).

So often the successes of yesterday fail in the marketplace today and often what works today may not be as effective tomorrow.

In business and indeed in life we need to have an open mind, be open to new ideas and know how to welcome change. We can only do this when we can recognise our failings and what we could have done better or differently.

It's not about thinking outside the square to reach your clients it's about becoming the square that they want to be a part of.

I know that my list of mistakes in marketing alone could fill countless books, but I remember hearing once that the one who has never failed has never truly tried.

Marketing is complex, let's not pretend otherwise.

It's easy to make mistakes when there are so many voices telling you how to do it, when to do it, where to do it and which way you should do it.

In a world full of guru's, it can be a valuable practice to step back, take a deep breath and just be still. Declutter your mind and focus back on the fundamentals of your reasons for being, your story and where you want to be.

There is freedom and release in this exercise and it won't be long before the clutter disappears and your mind is free to explore all of the unlimited opportunities that are before you.

In this blissful state, it can be a good opportunity to stop, reflect back on what worked, what didn't work and more importantly why?

One of the biggest mistakes I made in my businesses was trying to please all of the marketing and media sales people that would shower me with token gifts that were rarely ever free.

I would feel an obligation or a commitment to these people or companies because they had bombarded me with gifts, tickets, holidays and so on. A pretty good strategy by these companies in securing ongoing business.

Even though for the most part, these gifts were given in sincerity, they created an obligation that meant that I had surrendered my sovereignty and was losing control of my marketing and where I really wanted to be.

It's so easy to lose sight of the big picture when you are being derailed by the little distractions.

It's so important for you to know your marketing budget and your marketing strategy. I eventually learned the value of maintaining my focus and ultimately reclaimed my direction. I remembered that it was my business and my marketing dollars, not those who were keen to take them from me.

One of the first things I do with my clients, in my consulting business, after we have really established their story and where they want to be, is to look at their marketing budget and then cull where necessary.

We meet with their media representatives and have very honest and courageous conversations.

This can often make me very unpopular with media companies, but ultimately, it's not about them, it's about my clients and the outcomes they want and need.

Another huge mistake people are making now, is in dropping their traditional media strategies for less expensive social media options.

This is not a good idea unless you have one, very successful track record in social media. Television, radio and to a lesser degree press, are still powerful delivery systems and very cost effective when used correctly. When used in conjunction with your social media strategy, they can be even more effective.

Social media is here to stay, it can be very effective, but to dump traditional delivery systems on the advice of a social media "expert" is dangerous and even a little reckless.

Make intelligent decisions when it comes to your delivery systems and know where your ideal customer is and how to reach them.

In an article published on December 9, 2016 from the advertising industries AdAge, Coca-Cola Co. Global Chief Marketing Officer, Marcos de Quinto reportedly defended TV advertising, as providing the best bang for buck, while questioning the beverage giant's past digital spending practices. If Coke can learn these lessons, then so can we.

Marcos de Quinto stated, that TV is still "very, very critical for their business." During a presentation at a beverage industry conference in New York hosted by trade publication Beverage Digest, de Quinto showed a slide, declaring that "TV still offers the best ROI across media channels." The data on the slide was from 2014, however it did show Coca-Cola's TV investment returning $2.13 for every dollar spent on TV, compared with $1.26 for digital.

de Quinto went on to say, "We are very seriously trying to transform our company to make it a digital company, but it's not just to put ads in social media," he then showed a slide that stated: "Social media is the strategy for those who don't have a true digital strategy."

Social Media can be a minefield and a bottomless pit for your marketing budget. Remember not to get caught up in the frenzy and hype. Keep a level head and stay committed to your big picture marketing budget and strategy.

It takes time to build a social media community and depending on which platforms you decide to use; some journeys can be longer than others.

You also should really question, if search engines are where your marketing dollars should be going as well.

If you are relying on a customer to find you and to connect through a search engine, then you have truly failed at your marketing.

Should you list in search directories? Absolutely, if you want to reach the masses and if your marketing budget allows you the luxury, but the intelligent approach is to focus on building your brand.

Some industries have historically been more dependent upon search engines, than others. For example, a plumber, a painter or a pest controller would usually be found through a business directory, but it's a lucky dip. Have you seen how many listings exist in some of these categories? In some regions, it's needle in a hay stack status.

Engage with the heart of your customer or client and they won't even use a search engine. You will already have their loyalty and if your branding strategy has been effective, they will be searching your business by your name.

Not reaching the heart of your customer, is a critical error and this is the biggest mistake gripping the business world in the early days of the twenty first century.

If you don't take the longevity of your brand seriously, then go ahead and spend in search engines. If you want to build a long term business, market your brand, so that you in effect become a house hold name in your region and own your category. It's not expensive or hard, when you do it correctly.

One of the most frustrating things I see in marketing today, are business owners or managers who pull out of a strategy, halfway through because they aren't seeing the results they believe they should be seeing.

If you are trying to reach your potential customers through television or radio and you have never been in that space before, you have to accept the fact, that you most likely have very little awareness or credibility in the eyes and ears of your audience and you need to earn your place.

Based on my knowledge and experience in television and radio you need at least six months of consistent frequency, to begin to see a result. If the content is engaging, your patience will be rewarded. The more consistent you are in a particular space, the more effective your marketing will be.

If you can remember that, everything you do in marketing is all about building a relationship, then you will understand that consistent communication is critical to a successful outcome.

Remember, it's about heart engagement - that's what stands the test of time.

A huge mistake people make, is their eagerness to waste thousands of dollars on gimmicks. Gimmicks don't work and they can often insult the intelligence of your existing or future customers.

If it feels a little bit tacky or sleazy, then it's not a good idea for you or your brand.

The question to ask yourself is how would the heart of my ideal client respond to this?

Are you wasting money on beer holders, bottle openers or water bottles to win customers?

I hope not.

I personally accumulated twelve of these in the last year through various "promotional" presentations. They have all been taken to the recyclers and never used.

If you are sponsoring a sporting team as part of your strategy then branded water bottles make a lot of sense. The cost versus the impact for general marketing with these types of gimmicks is unrealistic in many instances.

One mistake I made early on in my business and marketing career was to lose sight of who I was trying to reach. I love marketing so much I would get swept away in all the potential delivery systems available. Even though there were less options available back then, there were still plenty of ways to waste money.

What I learnt from this mistake of trying to talk to everyone, all the time and in every instance, is that it rarely works. If you are talking to everyone, you are engaging no one.

One message at a time, speak to the heart of your customer and turn them into a client.

Decide on the delivery systems that are going to carry your story to the heart of your desired customer and remain committed to them for the duration of your strategy.

Choose no more than two social media platforms and combine these with your TV, radio and/or press strategies.

Own the space you are in before venturing off to conquer new audiences.

If you are going to invest in a marketing campaign, then make sure you are ready for the response from the marketplace. Learn to communicate your marketing activity to your entire team. Especially those on the front line of customer interaction.

Ensure that your customers' expectations are met at the very least, exceeded where ever possible.

Never allow yourself the embarrassment of underwhelming your customers.

Keep your website and other public digital platforms current and updated. I found in an audit of one of my clients, that they had pricing and information that was three years out of date.

So many people, simply tick a box when it comes to their marketing because they know they need to market, so they sign up to the first thing that comes along.

Don't be reactive when it comes to your marketing, be intentional because the attitude behind your marketing and how seriously you are will determine the outcome.

Just because a competitor has tried something out to the box doesn't mean you need to deviate from your strategy. Give things time and be patient.

It is almost impossible to be all things to all people all of the time. If that is your goal you will need very deep pockets and unlimited resources at your disposal.

Stay focused on your big picture and don't forget the heart of what it is you are doing. Always remember your why and stay true to the values of your brand!

Write it down, post it on your walls if you have to, but always remember the reasons why you set out on your journey.

Be realistic when projecting the outcomes you want to see and manage your expectations.

SHANE'S TIP

Knowing that it's ok to make a mistake is liberating, but don't let it become a cop out for making the same mistakes over and over.

Learn from your mistakes, this will provide you with an even greater advantage in the marketing world. If you can, learn from the mistakes of others - these will cost you much less!

Step 10
YOUR MOVE

Next Steps

The next step in your marketing journey is to really get serious about where you want to arrive on this journey you are on.

Will today be the day that you decide that you have a vision that is worth pursuing?

Or will you, like the masses have every good intention about where you want to be and then give into excuses and mediocracy?

Business can be tough, but it can also be easy and enjoyable too.

Your mindset will either be a launch pad open to unlimited possibilities or a prison, bound by rigid belief.

In a world of constant change and ever increasing uncertainty when was the last time you changed? When was the last time you took a step into the unknown and backed yourself?

For some change is the gateway to unlimited opportunities, for others it's another reason to complain or give up. Which one are you?

Are you the ostrich or the eagle? Do you choose to soar to the edge of known possibilities or is your head firmly planted in the sand.

What you have within you is the absolute abundance of unlimited potential to be, do or achieve whatever it is you want to be, do or achieve.

When will be your now moment?

When will you choose to break through rather than break down?

Business can be tough but it's often our mindsets that make it tougher.

Make today the day that you decide to embrace change and conquer your Everest.

Marketing can be a maze with no apparent way forward and this can become very frustrating. There is hope and there certainly is a light at the end of the tunnel. You and I are living in the most amazing time in known history. Never before have we had the array of tools available to us, like we have today, to reach our market.

Take a long hard look at where you are and be honest with yourself about how you feel about it.

Maybe you are happy with where you are and believe me, I truly hope this is the case for you!

Maybe you just want to tweak things and gain another perspective on what you are doing and that's a very healthy place to be in. Maybe you are a little lost, overwhelmed, distracted, confused or jaded by your marketing experiences? If so, why not make the commitment to your future and decide today that you will change what needs to be changed, fix what needs to be fixed, cull what needs to be culled and get to the heart of what it is that you are really all about.

What you project from your heart centre is what people see. It truly is.

The things you say and do can never mask the truth that is revealed by your heart. For out of your heart, flows the real you. For the heart is one with the soul and this is what people really see - every time.

There is a massive number of business owners who will miss these fundamental truths about marketing to the heart. Centering yourself at the core of your values.

These people will remain oblivious as to what matters the most to the heart of their customer and they will march on to the end of their journey without knowing the amazing power that lies within the truth. That it's really only ever about the heart's desires.

Let's face it, in many cases even ignorant marketing speaks to the heart of the issue. Whether it be a commercial for a new car, a new watch or a tropical escape. Clever marketers are targeting the hearts desires, so why shouldn't you do the same, coming from a position of sincerity and integrity.

Each year I take on a limited number of new consulting clients and why shouldn't we work on your business together?

My disclaimer is that I won't work with everyone who applies to work with me and yes there is an application process.

The reason I have an application form for potential clients, is that I know who I want as my perfect client and if we aren't aligned in our thinking, values and direction, I'm unable to truly add value to your business.

Many of my clients, now engage me for a minimum of two years and to be honest, in some cases this can be a lot longer.

Your business is a living entity and things change, technologies evolve and improve and so does the marketplace and for this reason we consistently review and strategise towards the ideal predetermined destination.

Go forward follow your passion, believe in your vision and be epic!

Engage with me and let's create your Brand and Marketing with Heart.

CHECKLIST

1. You know your budget for the next 24 months [ ]

2. You and your team clearly know your vision and values [ ]

3. Your vision and values statement is in easy view for both your team and your customers to read [ ]

4. Your 12 month marketing plan and strategy is written down and understood [ ]

5. You have created your ideal client profile [ ]

ABOUT THE AUTHOR

Shane's approach is different, it is sensible and it comes from years of business and marketing experience that has seen him work with some of the largest companies in Australia.

After building his own successful businesses through effective and creative marketing strategies, Shane pursued his passion for marketing with a successful career in television and radio marketing and later the digital space.

His understanding and sensitivity to the heart of the individual, truly sets him apart. He is highly sought after as an independent marketing consultant, often having a waiting list of clients wanting to work with him.

Shane McLeay is really about heart felt, values based, intelligent marketing and his client's testimonials are a tribute to the success of his simple, yet effective philosophies that really get to the heart of it all.

ABOUT HEART MARKETING

In a world that longs for something more, we need to look beyond the cookie cutter marketing strategies, the data and the statistics and focus on the heart of who it is we are really trying to reach.

People value personal growth, yet their intelligence is constantly insulted with tacky and irrelevant marketing messages.

People today want to feel worthy and validated, yet their self esteem is targeted and attacked through insensitive marketing campaigns.

People value their connectivity to that which is greater than just self, people today long for spiritual connection and in business today these fundamental needs are so often overlooked.

Heart Marketing is about speaking to the heart of the individual you are wanting to reach. Through Heart Marketing, Shane McLeay brings his successful business and marketing knowledge and combines it with his sensitivity to spirituality and the heartbeat of the people.

Heart Marketing really does get to the heart of some important issues in marketing today and will be a valuable tool to anyone wanting to make a difference with their marketing.

www.ingramcontent.com/pod-product-compliance
Lightning Source LLC
Chambersburg PA
CBHW051314220526
45468CB00004B/1339